Presented to

_____

from

_____

on

_____

Table Graces for the Family

THOMAS NELSON PUBLISHERS

Nashville • Camden • New York

Second printing

Revised Edition
Copyright © 1984 by Thomas Nelson, Inc.

Original Edition
Copyright © 1964 by Thomas Nelson, Inc.

Selections for the original edition of *Table Graces for the Family* were made by Marjorie Ingzel.

Published in Nashville, Tennessee, by Thomas Nelson, Inc. and distributed in Canada by Lawson Falle, Ltd., Cambridge, Ontario.

Scripture quotations in this text are from the NEW KING JAMES VERSION of the Bible. Copyright © 1979, 1980, 1982, Thomas Nelson, Inc., Publishers.

Library of Congress Cataloging in Publication Data
Main entry under title:

Table graces for the family.

Summary: A collection of graces for everyday and for special occasions culled from the Bible, prayer books, literature, and other sources.
1. Grace at meals—Christianity. 2. Family—Prayerbooks and devotions—English. [1. Grace at meals. 2. Prayer books and devotions]
BV283.G7T28   1984   242'.72   84-11535
ISBN 0-8407-5369-1

ACKNOWLEDGEMENTS

Reprinted by permission of the copyright owners, all rights reserved:

Concordia Publishing House—From THE CHILDREN'S HYMNAL: first grace, 20; second grace, 22; first grace, 31. Copyright © 1955. Used by permission.

Fleming H. Revell—From A BOOK OF TABLE GRACES by John Lewis Sandlin: first grace, 92; second grace, 92; first grace, 93; second grace, 93; second grace 94; second grace 98; second grace, 102; first grace, 106. Copyright © 1963 by Fleming H. Revell Company. Published by Fleming H. Revell Company. Used by permission.

Girl Scouts of the U.S.A., New York— From THE DITTY BAG: "Hark to the Chimes," 78. Copyright © 1946; From SING TOGETHER: "Scottish Grace" and "Allelujah," 78, 79. Copyright © 1936 by Girl Scouts of the U.S.A. Reprinted by permission of the Girl Scouts of the U.S.A.

Holt, Rinehart, and Winston—From GRACE BEFORE MEALS compiled by William A. Nyce and Hubert Bunyea: first grace, 90; second grace, 96. Copyright © 1911, 1939 by Holt, Rinehart and Winston. Reprinted by permission of Holt, Rinehart and Winston Publishers.

New Century Publishers—Reprinted from CHILDREN'S PRAYERS FROM OTHER LANDS by Dorothy Gladys Spicer Fraser: all prayers, 45-48. Copyright © 1954. By permission of New Century Publishers, Inc. in Piscataway, NJ.

The Upper Room—From TABLE GRACES: Prayer by H.A. Boaz, first grace, 32; adapted from prayer by H.B. Milward, first grace, 104; adapted from prayer by Clara M. Bogue, first grace, 121. Published by The Upper Room, Nashville, TN. Reprinted by permission.

Vineyard Books—Adapted from prayers by Avery Brooke in YOUTH TALKS WITH GOD: second grace, 50; second grace, 52; grace, 54. Permission granted by Vineyard Books, Inc., P.O. Box 3315, Noroton, CT 06820.

In a book of this type, there are inevitably numerous copyright owners. Every effort has been made to trace and contact all the copyright owners. Inadvertant omissions, if called to the publisher's attention, will be noted in future editions.

Contents

Introduction

The Bible tells us that "the effective, fervent prayer of a righteous man avails much" (James 5:16). This is true in any context, but nowhere is it more important than in the home. Faith and love begin at home, and so this is where prayer must first be emphasized.

Traditionally, mealtime has been the occasion designated for family prayer. Since this is still the time that most families gather, it continues to be important to recognize God's grace and generosity in this setting. This book has been designed to help the family in doing just that.

In order for family prayer to be effective, we feel that there are a few guidelines which should be followed. We have tried to keep these in mind while compiling the prayers included in this book.

First, prayer should be *short*. If the grace or prayer is too long, it will lose the attention of the family and become a source of frustration rather than enjoyment.

Second, prayer should be *simple*. The Lord's prayer is an excellent example of prayer that is short and to the point. Even young children can easily understand what is being said and they can join in the worship.

Prayer should also be *direct* and *sincere*. We should pray directly to the Lord and not to those around us. It should also be obvious that we mean what we say and are not merely reciting words.

Prayer should be *regular*, and most important, it should be an offering *from the entire family*. What better way to knit a close family than to pray consistently to God as a family?

This book has been written in such a manner as to provide a variety of options for the format of prayers at meals—everything from traditional old prayers to contemporary prayers for children and special occasions.

We hope that this book will be of good use to your family as you pray and worship together.

The Editors

The Lord's Prayer

Our Father which art in heaven, Hallowed be thy
   name.
Thy kingdom come. Thy will be done in earth, as it is
   in heaven.
Give us this day our daily bread.
And forgive us our debts, as we forgive our debtors.
And lead us not into temptation, but deliver us from
   evil:
For thine is the kingdom, and the power, and the
   glory, forever.
Amen.

Matthew 6:9-13 KJV

Part I

Traditional Graces

General

Come, Lord Jesus, be our guest;
And let these gifts to us be blessed. Amen.

Bless, O Father, Your gifts to our use and us to Your
service; for Christ's sake. Amen.

Book of Common Prayer

We, ask You, Father, to be present at our table, to
bless this food, and to make us truly thankful for all
Your mercies. Amen.

Lord, we pray that You will be merciful to us and watch over us. Bless this food to our use and draw us closer to You. Through the name of our Lord and Savior Jesus Christ. Amen.

We accept, Lord, these gifts from You because You are the giver of every good and perfect gift. While receiving Your blessings, teach us clearly that all we have—including our very lives—is because of Your generosity. In Christ's name we pray. Amen.

Our loving heavenly Father, as we sit around this table, our hearts unite in praising You for the blessings of this day. Amen.

Lord of our salvation, from whom alone all good things come, we ask You to satisfy all our needs from Your bounty, and we thank You for these, Your gifts. Amen.

Dear Lord, we praise you for the love in our family and we ask Your blessings on us as we prepare to eat together. We thank You for this food and for the one who has prepared it. Be with us as we strive to serve You better. In Jesus' name we pray. Amen.

As we gather at this table, we rejoice that You know our weaknesses. You know that hands, head, and heart are often weary, and we ask You to strengthen us with this food so that we may be active in Your service. Amen.

For these and all Your mercies, we praise Your holy name. Amen.

Help us remember, Lord, Your tender mercies and Your loving-kindnesses which have always existed. Because of Your mercy, think of us, teach us, and make us thankful for these blessings which are now spread before us. Amen.

Almighty God, we thank You for every good and perfect gift and above all for the gift of Your Son Jesus Christ, our Lord, who is the bread to our souls, as this food is to our bodies. Amen.

Gracious God, bless this food which we are about to eat in Christ's name. Amen.

For this good fellowship, our Father, we thank You. We praise You for this nourishing food, Your loving care, and our family. Blend our hearts as we break bread together so that happiness may dwell in our home. Supply us with Your love, Lord, for the sake of Your Son, in whose name we pray. Amen.

As You fed the hungry crowd by the Sea of Galilee, so also feed us, Lord. Refresh our bodies, and bring peace to our souls. We ask this in the name of Jesus, who is the Bread of Life. Amen.

Our God and Father, help those of us together here to be of one mind and one heart, united in truth, peace, faith, and love. May we together glorify You, our Lord and Savior, and receive with gratitude these gifts. Amen.

Great God, Giver of all good,
Accept our praise, and bless our food.
Grace, health, and strength to us afford,
Through Jesus Christ, our blessed Lord. Amen.

We thank You, Father, for these gifts of Your grace. May they strengthen us to live as Your servants and so fulfill Your perfect divine plan. Amen.

Heavenly Father, please listen to Your children's prayer. Grant us pardon for our sins and replenish us with Your peace which You know we need. May this food strengthen our bodies to Your honor and glory. Amen.

For feeding us at this time, we heartily thank You, most merciful Father. Please feed our souls likewise with the meat that does not perish, but lasts forever, so that we, being fed both in body and soul, may always do that which is pleasant in Your sight. Through Jesus Christ our Lord. Amen.

Lord, we thank You for the joys of life, for our daily bread, which nourishes our bodies, and for the night of sleep which brings tranquility and strength for the duties of a new day. Amen.

Be present at our table, Lord;
Be here and everywhere adored.
Thy creatures bless, and grant that we
May feast in paradise with Thee.

John Wesley

We thank You, Lord, for our daily bread. May it strengthen and refresh our bodies. We pray that You will feed our souls with Your heavenly grace, through Jesus Christ, our Lord. Amen.

Almighty God, heavenly Father, we give You thanks for all Your gifts and goodness; and we pray that as You feed our bodies, also graciously keep our souls pure in the true faith. Through Jesus Christ our Lord. Amen.

Most gracious God, we give You humble and heartfelt thanks for the great mercy which You have given to us. Help us to show our gratitude, not only with our words, but in our ways, by giving ourselves to Your service, and by walking before You in holiness and righteousness all our days. Through Jesus Christ, our Lord, to whom, with You and the Holy Ghost, be all honor and glory. Amen.

Give us grateful hearts, our Father, for all Thy
mercies, and make us mindful of the needs of others; through Jesus Christ our Lord. Amen.

Book of Common Prayer

Bless, Father, all those for whom we would pray.
Guard them this day, and may all our hearts join in
praising You for Your great love shown in this supply of our daily needs. Amen.

Heavenly Father, grant Your blessing
On the food before us spread,
All our tongues are now confessing
By Your hand alone we're fed. Amen.

As a shepherd leads his flock, so, Lord, we pray for You to lead us in the paths of righteousness for Your name's sake. As we eat this food which You have provided, may we remember that You have prepared a table for us, and goodness and mercy shall follow us all the days of our lives if we obey Your voice and follow Your leading. Grant, Lord, that we may dwell in the house of the Lord forever. Amen.

Lord God, heavenly Father, bless us and these Your gifts which we receive from Your bountiful goodness; through Jesus Christ our Lord. Amen.

We thank You, O God our Father, for Your watchful care over us. Protect us from all evil and harm, and guard and guide us in all our ways. Bless this food to our use and us to Your service. In Jesus' name. Amen.

Gracious God, may the food we are about to eat strengthen our bodies; and may Your Holy Spirit strengthen and refresh our souls; through Jesus Christ. Amen.

Lord, bless these gifts of Your providence to our use, and give us grateful hearts for all Your mercies to us and to everyone. Amen.

The earth is full of Your goodness, Lord; You give to all their sustenance in due time. You open Your hands, and they are filled with all that is good. Your glory shall endure forever, and we shall rejoice in Your works. Amen.

Heavenly Father, make us thankful to You and mindful of others, as we receive these blessings; in Jesus' name. Amen.

O give thanks unto the Lord, for He is good, His mercy endureth forever. He giveth food to all flesh, He giveth to the beast his food, and to the young ravens which cry. The Lord taketh pleasure in them that fear Him, in those that hope in His mercy. Amen.

Martin Luther

Help us, Lord, to seek first the kingdom of God and Your righteousness, and to know, therefore, that we shall never lack any good thing. We thank You again for all these blessings which You have provided. Amen.

Bless us, Lord, in what we are about to receive, and make us truly thankful; for Jesus Christ's sake. Amen.

Each gift of Yours, dear Lord, helps us to learn how boundless is Your supply, and we go from day to day upheld by Your almighty arm. Please accept our thanks for Jesus' sake. Amen.

Father, on You we place our every care; we live through You who knows our every need. O, feed us with Your grace and give our souls this day the living bread. Amen.

As we bow before You, heavenly Father, we realize that Your love has no limit, and we want to rest in this love throughout the remainder of the day. May the renewed strength obtained from this food be spent in Your service. Amen.

We thank You, our Father, that You who clothe the lilies of the field and feed the birds of the air will also care for us. We know it is by Your graciousness that we are clothed and fed. Amen.

You open Your hand, O Lord,
The earth is filled with good;
Teach us with thankful hearts to take
From You our daily food. Amen.

We give You hearty thanks, our Father, for our daily blessings, and we pray that You will continue Your loving-kindness to us. Through Christ our Lord. Amen.

Accept our thanks, O Lord, for these Your gifts. Make us truly thankful for all Your mercies now and forevermore. In the name of Your beloved Son. Amen.

Morning _____

For the night's rest, the morning meal, the new day, and all the blessings it may bring, we give You grateful thanks, our Father. Help us to serve You by serving others; through Jesus Christ our Lord. Amen.

Help us, our Father, to keep watch over our thoughts and words this day. Help us to be obedient to Christ our Lord. May we remember that this is the day which the Lord has made, and let us rejoice and be glad in it. As we eat and drink, may we remember that You are the giver of every good and perfect gift. Amen.

We thank You, Father, for this new day which You are giving us, and for all it brings to remind us of Your love. May this food strengthen us for our duties, and may our lives today be for Your glory and honor. Amen.

May this day bring to us a renewed sense of Your great love and wonderful kindness. Grant us grace, Lord, for the tasks of the day, and strengthen our souls as this food will strengthen our bodies. Amen.

Since it is of Your mercy, O gracious Father, that another day is added to our lives, we dedicate our souls and our bodies to You and to Your service in the hours ahead. We know that You will strengthen us, so that as we grow in age, we may grow in grace, and in an understanding of our Lord and Savior Jesus Christ. Amen.

33

Each morning new mercies dawn. O teach us, Lord, how to begin and end each day with praise and prayer. May the food which has been prepared for us make us mindful of Your constant love and sustaining grace. Amen.

Our hearts worship You this morning. You have kept us in safety throughout the night, and we are thankful, Father, for Your protecting care. We thank You for this food, and may the strength we receive from it be spent in Your service. We pray through Jesus. Amen.

Lord, we know that Your steadfast love never ceases. We thank You for the new mercies that each morning brings. You are our portion and we will hope in You. Bless us this day. We pray through Christ. Amen.

Lord, your mercies surround us and we are grateful. Grant that our service to You may increase. Let us today demonstrate our gratitude by doing those things that are well pleasing to You. For we pray through Jesus. Amen.

We give You thanks, O heavenly Father, who has kept us through the night. We pray that You will guide us this day to serve You better. May we always praise Your name. Through Jesus Christ our Lord. Amen.

Grant us, Lord, to live this day in gladness and peace. We pray that we will overcome the temptations of the day and truly live for You. We praise You for Your guidance in our lives and pray that we will continually strive to be more like Christ. We pray through His name. Amen.

Lord, we thank You for the gift of sleep, for our health and strength, for the beginning of another day, and for our daily food. We pray that we will use the new opportunities for work and service to their fullest. Help us to keep our trust and faith in You. We praise You for the gift of Your Son. It is in His name that we pray. Amen.

Most holy and ever-loving God, we thank You
once more for the quiet rest of the night that has
gone by, for the new promise that has come with
this fresh morning, and for the hope of this day.
While we have slept, the world in which we live has
swept on, and we have rested under the shadow of
Your love. May we trust You this day for all the
needs of the body, the soul, and the spirit. Give us
this day our daily bread. Amen.

Robert Collyer

Grant that we may realize that the blessings You
give us here are but an indication of the blessings of
the life to come. May we give ourselves into Your
keeping this day. For we pray in Jesus' name. Amen.

37

You have mercifully kept us through the night; how wonderful is Your continued goodness. Protect us this day. Guide and assist us in all our thoughts, words, and actions. Make us willing to do what you wish. In the matchless name of Jesus we pray. Amen.

Bless all who worship You, from sunrise to sunset. Of Your goodness, give us; with Your love, inspire us; by Your spirit, guide us; by Your power, protect us; in Your mercy, receive us now and always. Amen.

Our Father, bless our evening meal. Forgive all that You have seen wrong in us today, in thought or word or deed. And keep us this night in Your holy care. Through Jesus. Amen.

Father, continue Your gracious watch over us this night. Make us ever mindful of Your protection and grateful for these blessings before us, through Jesus Christ in whose name we pray. Amen.

Abide with us, O good Lord, through the night — guarding, keeping, guiding, sustaining, and with Your love, gladdening us. May we ever live in You. Through Jesus Christ our Lord we pray. Amen.

Lord, we thank You for Your love and Your plan of salvation. We ask Your forgiveness for all that we have done wrong today. Please help us as we try to be more like our Savior. Thank You for the food we have before us now. May we be strengthened by it in order to serve You better. For we pray through Christ. Amen.

As we lift up our hearts in thanksgiving for the blessings of the day that has passed, we pray that You will watch over us this night, and bring us to yet another day to work for You. We praise You for Your generosity toward us, and we pray that You will accept our thanks for this food. In Jesus' name. Amen.

Create in us clean hearts, O Lord, and renew a right spirit within us. We thank You that You supply all our wants and needs. Please help us to desire only that which is well-pleasing to You. We thank You now for this food we have before us. In Christ's name we pray. Amen.

We praise You, Lord, for the mercies of yet another day. We pray that You will accept our evening prayer of thanks for these provisions of Your love. Be with us tonight and bring us into a new day tomorrow. In Jesus' name. Amen.

Father, we thank You for the joy that makes our hearts glad—the joy of the Lord which is our strength. We thank You now for the food You have given to sustain us. We know it is from Your hand that we are fed. We pray these things through Your Son. Amen.

Gracious and loving Father, receive us this night for Jesus' sake. We offer to You a prayer of thanksgiving. Bless any good thing we have done today. Forgive us if we have spoken or done anything wrong against anyone. Graciously watch over us tonight. Please care for all our friends. We ask these things through Christ. Amen.

Lord Jesus, we praise You for the beauties of this day. We thank You for Your blessings and Your love. We thank You for our home and the joys we share here. Bless us this night as we eat together. For we pray in Your Son's name. Amen.

We give thanks unto Thee, heavenly Father, through Jesus Christ, Thy dear Son, that Thou hast this day so graciously protected us, and we beseech Thee to forgive us all our sins, and the wrong which we have done, and by Thy great mercy defend us from all the perils and dangers of this night. Into Thy hands we commend our bodies and souls, and all that is ours. Let Thy holy angel have charge concerning us, that the wicked one have no power over us.

Martin Luther

All praise to Thee, my God, this night,
For all the blessings of the light:
Keep me, O keep me, King of kings,
Beneath Thine own almighty wings.

Forgive me, Lord, for Thy dear Son,
The ill that I this day have done;
That with the world, myself, and Thee,
I, ere I sleep, at peace may be.

O may my soul on Thee repose,
And with sweet sleep mine eyelids close;
Sleep that shall me more vigorous make
To serve my God when I awake.

O when shall I, in endless day,
For ever chase dark sleep away,
And hymns divine with angels sing,
All praise to Thee, eternal King?

Bishop Thomas Ken (1709)

...The blessing of God...rest upon all those who have been kind to us, have cared for us, have worked for us, have served us, and have shared our bread with us at this table. Our merciful God, reward all of them in your own way...for Yours is the glory and the honor for ever. Amen.

Egypt

Each time we eat, may we remember God's love. Amen.

China

Thank you, kind Father, for giving us food to make our bodies grow stronger. Dear God, teach us to share with others what we ourselves have. Amen.

China

O God, who makes a thousand flowers to blow,
Who makes both grains and fruits to grow,
Hear our prayer:
Bless this food
And bring us peace. Amen.

Netherlands

Come, God be our guest;
May our food thus be blessed. Amen.

Germany

Thank You, O God so good,
For today's bread.
Thank You for Your thoughtfulness,
Thank You for Your love. Amen.

Switzerland and Belgium

We gather for this meal
And together we pray;
Thank You, God,
For those who have made it ready for us.
Dear God, make us all
Parts of Your great family. Amen.

France

For the beauty of our country paths and roads,
For today and for tomorrow;
For the bread which we eat;
For our good friends, too,
We thank You, God. Amen.

France

Father, who feeds the small sparrows, give us our
bread and feed all our brothers. Amen.

France

47

Let us in peace eat the food that God has provided for us. Praise be to God for all His gifts. Amen.

Lebanon

May the abundance of this table never fail and never be less, thanks to the blessings of God, who has fed us and satisfied our needs. To Him be glory for ever. Amen.

Lebanon

Thank You for the world so sweet,
Thank You for the food we eat,
Thank You for the birds that sing,
Thank You, God, for everything. Amen.

E. Rutter Leatham

O Lord, I thank You for the food
You have given me to do me good:
Be pleased, O Lord, to bless the same,
I ask it in the Savior's name. Amen.

We thank You, loving Father,
For all Your tender care,
For food and clothes and shelter,
And all Your world so fair. Amen.

God is great, and God is good,
And we thank Him for our food.
By His hand we all are fed.
Give us, Lord, our daily bread. Amen.

O God, please be with me through this day. Fill my heart with love for You and everyone I meet. If someone is sad, help me to comfort him. If someone is unfair, help me to forgive him. If someone is angry, help me to be patient with him. If someone especially needs love, help me to love him. And when things go wrong today, let me remember to ask Your help. In Jesus' name. Amen.

For every cup and plateful,
God make us truly grateful. Amen.

All things bright and beautiful,
All creatures great and small,
All things wise and wonderful:
The Lord God made them all.

He gave us eyes to see them,
And lips that we might tell,
How great is God Almighty,
Who has made all things well. Amen.

Cecil Francis Alexander (1818-1895)

Dear Lord, thank You for giving me another day. Help me to concentrate on my work at school, to be respectful to my teachers, to be fair when I play games, to be obedient to my parents, to be a willing helper at home, and to be kind to my friends. Help me to make this day more pleasant for everyone by being cheerful. Please bless my family and all those I love. In Jesus' name. Amen.

O Lord, I thank You for the sky and sea and air, for all the places I know and love and the places I have not yet seen. I thank You for my friends and family and for the people I know who teach Your love to me by their example. I thank You for the chance to learn and grow and change. I thank You for loving me even when I fail You and for always letting me try again. Amen.

Lord, I thank You that You give
The daily bread by which I live:
O bless the food I now partake,
And save my soul for Jesus' sake. Amen.

All this day Your hand has led me,
And I thank You for Your care:
You have warmed me, clothed and fed me,
Listen to my evening prayer. Amen.

O God, bless all the people that I love at home, in school, and far away. Guide them by day and by night and keep them always under Your loving care. And, Lord, bless also the people I don't love the way I should. Teach me to love them and understand them in spite of our differences. Help me to forgive those who act badly toward me and especially bless them because they need Your love as well as mine. In Jesus' name. Amen.

—————————————————————————— Part II

Prayers from the Bible

The LORD bless you and keep you;
The LORD make His face shine upon you,
And be gracious to you;
The LORD lift up His countenance upon you,
And give you peace.

Numbers 6:24-26

Blessed are You, LORD God of Israel,
    our Father, forever and ever....
Both riches and honor come from You,
And You reign over all.
In Your hand is power and might;
In Your hand it is to make great
And to give strength to all.
Now therefore, our God,
We thank You
And praise Your glorious name.

1 Chronicles 29:10,12-13

Make a joyful shout to the LORD,
    all you lands!
Serve the LORD with gladness;
Come before His presence with singing.
Know that the LORD, He is God;
It is He who has made us,
    and not we ourselves;
We are His people
    and the sheep of His pasture.
Enter into His gates with thanksgiving,
And into His courts with praise.
Be thankful to Him
    and bless His name.
For the LORD is good;
His mercy is everlasting,
And His truth endures to all
    generations.

Psalm 100

Bless the LORD, O my soul;
And all that is within me,
  bless His holy name!
Bless the LORD, O my soul,
And forget not all His benefits.

Psalm 103:1-2

Oh, that men would give thanks to the
  LORD for His goodness,
And for His wonderful works to the
  children of men!
For He satisfies the longing soul,
And fills the hungry soul with
  goodness.

Psalm 107:8-9

Oh, give thanks to the Lord,
    for He is good!
For His mercy endures forever....
Who remembered us in our lowly state,
    For His mercy endures forever...
Who gives food to all flesh,
    For His mercy endures forever.
Oh, give thanks to the God of heaven!
    For His mercy endures forever.

Psalm 136:1,23,25-26

The eyes of all look expectantly to You,
And You give them their food in due season.
You open Your hand
And satisfy the desire of every living thing.

Psalm 145:15-16

Praise the LORD! Praise the LORD, O my soul!...
Happy is he who has the God of Jacob
   for his help,
Whose hope is in the LORD his God....
Who executes justice for the oppressed,
Who gives food to the hungry.
The LORD gives freedom to the
   prisoners.

Psalm 146:1,5,7

Sing to the LORD with thanksgiving;
Sing praises on the harp to our God,
Who covers the heavens with clouds,
Who prepares rain for the earth,
Who makes grass to grow on the
   mountains.
He gives to the beast its food,
And to the young ravens that cry.

Psalm 147:7-9

60

But He answered and said, "It is written, 'Man shall not live by bread alone, but by every word that proceeds from the mouth of God.' "

Matthew 4:4

Ask and it will be given to you;
   seek, and you will find;
   knock, and it will be opened to you.
For everyone who asks receives,
   and he who seeks finds,
   and to him who knocks it will be opened.

Matthew 7:7-8

Do not labor for the food which perishes, but for the food which endures to everlasting life, which the Son of Man will give you, because God the Father has set His seal on Him....For the bread of God is He who comes down from heaven and gives life to the world....I am the bread of life. He who comes to Me shall never hunger, and he who believes in Me shall never thirst.

John 6:27,33,35

And whatever you ask in My name, that I will do, that the Father may be glorified in the Son.

John 14:13

The grace of the Lord Jesus Christ, and the love of God, and the communion of the Holy Spirit be with you all. Amen.

2 Corinthians 13:14

———————————————————— Part III

Prayers of Noted People

Church Leaders

Watch Thou, dear Lord, with those who wake, or watch, or weep to-night, and give Thine angels charge over those who sleep. Tend Thy sick ones, O Lord Christ. Rest Thy weary ones. Bless Thy dying ones. Soothe Thy suffering ones. Pity Thine afflicted ones. Shield Thy joyous ones. And all, for Thy Love's sake. Amen.

St. Augustine (354)

I bind unto myself today
The power of God to hold and lead
His eye to watch, His might to stay,
His ear to hearken to my need;
The wisdom of my God to teach,
His hand to guide, His shield to ward;
The word of God to give me speech,
His heavenly host to be my guard.

St. Patrick (389-461)

Grant, O our God, that we may know Thee, love Thee, and rejoice in Thee; and if in this life we cannot do these things fully, grant that we may at least progress in them from day to day; for Christ's sake.

St. Anselm

Lord, make me an instrument of Thy peace:
Where there is hatred, let me sow love;
Where there is injury, pardon;
Where there is discord, union;
Where there is doubt, faith;
Where there is despair, hope;
Where there is darkness, light;
Where there is sadness, joy.

St. Francis of Assissi (1182-1226)

Day by day, dear Lord,
Of Thee three things I pray:
To see Thee more clearly,
Love Thee more dearly,
Follow Thee more nearly,
Day by day.

Richard of Chichester (circa 1197-1253)

The things, good Lord, that we pray for, give us
grace to work for.

Sir Thomas Moore (1478-1535)

Almighty God, who hath placed us in this world
and from whom we daily receive so many blessings,
grant that we may so pass our time as to regard our
end and hasten towards the goal. O grant that the
benefits and blessings by which Thou invitest us to
Thyself may not become snares to hold us to this
world, but may stimulate us to fear Thy name and
appreciate Thy mercy, so that we may thus know
Thee to be our God, and strive on our part to be
Thy people, and so to consecrate ourselves and all
our service to Thee, that Thy name may be glorified
in us, through Christ our Lord. Amen.

John Calvin (1509-1564)

Be gracious to all our friends and neighbors.
Bless our relations with the best of Thy blessings,
with Thy fear and love. Preserve us from our ene-
mies, and reconcile them both to us and to Thyself.

John Wesley (1703-1791)

Let Thy blessing rest upon us of this family. In
every condition secure our hearts to Thyself, and
make us ever to approve ourselves sincere and faithful in Thy service.

John Wesley (1703-1791)

O Lord of heaven, and earth, and sea,
To Thee all praise and glory be!
How shall we show our love to Thee,
    Giver of all?
For peaceful homes, and healthful days,
For all the blessings earth displays,
We owe Thee thankfulness and praise,
    Giver of all!

Bishop Christopher Wordsworth (1807-1885)

O Lord God, give us grace to set a good example
to all amongst whom we live, to be just and true in
all our dealings, to be strict and conscientious in
the discharge of every duty, pure and temperate in
all enjoyment, kind and charitable and courteous
toward all men; that so the mind of Jesus Christ
may be formed in us, and all men take knowledge of
us that we are His disciples; through the same
Jesus Christ our Lord.

Dean Vaughan (1816-1897)

The prayers I make will then be sweet indeed,
If Thou the spirit give by which I pray;
My unassisted heart is barren clay,
That of its native self can nothing feed.
Of good and pious works Thou art the seed
That quickens only where Thou say'st it may.
Unless Thou show to us Thine own true way,
No man can find it; Father, Thou must lead.
Do Thou then breathe those thoughts into my mind
By which such virtue may in me be bred
That in Thy holy footsteps I may tread;
The fetters of my tongue do Thou unbind
That I may have the power to sing of Thee,
And sound Thy praises everlastingly.

Michelangelo (1475-1564)

O LORD, that lends me life,
Lend me a heart replete with thankfulness!

William Shakespeare (1565-1616)

He was the Word, that spake it:
He took the bread and brake it;
And what that Word did make it,
I do believe and take it.

John Donne (1572-1631)

Thou hast given so much to me,
Give one thing more, a grateful heart,
Not thankful when it pleaseth me,
As if Thy blessings had spare days;
But such a heart, whose pulse may be
    Thy praise.

George Herbert (1593-1633)

Let us with a gladsome mind
Praise the Lord for He is kind;
For His mercies aye endure,
Ever faithful, ever sure.

All things living He doth feed,
His full hand supplies their need:
For His mercies aye endure,
Ever faithful, ever sure.

John Milton (1608-1674)

The Lord my pasture shall prepare,
And feed me with a shepherd's care
His presence shall my wants supply,
And guard me with a watchful eye.

Joseph Addison (1672-1719)

Make us to remember, O God, that every day is
Thy gift, and ought to be used according to Thy
command; through Jesus Christ our Lord.

Samuel Johnson (1709-1784)

O Thou, who kindly dost provide
For every creature's want!
We bless Thee, God of nature wide,
For all Thy goodness lent:
And, if it please Thee, heavenly Guide,
May never worse be sent;
But, whether granted or denied,
Lord, bless us with content!

Robert Burns (1759-1796)

We must praise Thy goodness, that Thou hast left
nothing undone to draw us to Thyself. But one
thing we ask of Thee, our God, not to cease Thy
work in our improvement. Let us tend towards
Thee, no matter by what means, and be fruitful in
good works, for the sake of Jesus Christ our Lord.
Amen.

Ludwig Van Beethoven (1770-1827)

He prayest best, who loveth best
All things both great and small;
For the dear God who loveth us,
He made and loveth all.

Samuel Taylor Coleridge (1772-1834)

For flowers that bloom about our feet,
   Father, we thank Thee;
For tender grass so fresh and sweet,
   Father, we thank Thee;
For song of bird and hum of bee,
For all things fair we hear or see,
Father in heaven, we thank Thee.

For this new morning with its light,
   Father, we thank Thee;
For rest and shelter of the night,
   Father, we thank Thee;
For health and food, for love and friends,
For everything Thy goodness sends,
Father in heaven, we thank Thee.

                Ralph Waldo Emerson (1803-1882)

I shout before Him in my plenitude
Of light and warmth, of hope and wealth and
   food;
Ascribing all good to the Only Good.

                   Christina Rossetti (1830-1894)

Speak, Lord, for Thy servant heareth.
Grant us ears to hear,
Eyes to see,
Wills to obey,
Hearts to love;
Then declare what Thou wilt,
Reveal what Thou wilt,
Command what Thou wilt,
Demand what Thou wilt.

                   Christina Rossetti (1830-1894)

Part IV

Prayers from Music

HARK TO THE CHIMES

Deliberately, as the chimes

Hark to the chimes, Come bow thy head.

We thank thee, God, For this good bread.

SCOTTISH GRACE

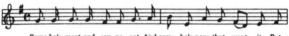

Some ha'e meat and can-na eat, And some ha'e none that want it, But

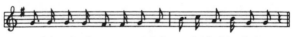

we ha'e meat and we can eat, And so the Lord be thank-et.

THE BOARD IS SPREAD

Morn - ing
Noon - time } is here, the board is spread,
Eve - ning

Thanks be to God, Who gives us bread.

ALLELUJAH

Bless this day, bless those here,
Come O Lord, share this hour;
May our lives glow with peace,
Blest with love and Your power.
Friendship and love may they bloom and grow
Bloom and grow forever.
Bless our friends, bless this food,
Bless all mankind forever.

To be sung to the tune of *Edelweis*

ABIDE WITH ME

Abide with me—fast falls the eventide,
The darkness deepens—Lord with me abide;
When other helpers fail and comforts flee,
Help of the helpless, O abide with me!

Swift to its close ebbs out life's little day,
Earth's joys grow dim, its glories pass away;
Change and decay in all around I see—
O Thou who changest not, abide with me!

I need Thy presence ev'ry passing hour—
What but Thy grace can foil the tempter's pow'r?
Who like Thyself my guide and stay can be?
Thru cloud and sunshine, O abide with me!

Hold Thou Thy word before my closing eyes,
Shine thru the gloom and point me to the skies;
Heav'n's morning breaks and earth's vain shadows
    flee—
In life, in death, O Lord, abide with me!

Henry F. Lyte (1793-1847)

ALL PEOPLE THAT ON EARTH DO DWELL

All people that on earth do dwell,
Sing to the Lord with cheerful voice;
Him serve with fear, His praise forth-tell,
Come ye before Him and rejoice.

Know that the Lord is God indeed:
Without our aid He did us make;
We are His folk, He doth us feed, and
For His sheep He doth us take.

O enter then His gates with praise,
Approach with joy His courts unto;
Praise, laud and bless His name always,
For it is seemly so to do.

For why? the Lord our God is good,
His mercy is forever sure;
His truth at all times firmly stood,
And shall from age to age endure.

From Psalm 100
Attr. to William Kethe, late 16th century—alt.

DAY IS DYING IN THE WEST

Day is dying in the west,
Heaven is touching earth with rest;
Wait and worship while the night
Sets her evening lamps alight
  Thro' all the sky.

While the deep'ning shadows fall,
Hearts of Love, enfolding all,
Thro' the glory and the grace
Of the stars that veil Thy face,
  Our hearts ascend.

Refrain:
Holy, holy, holy
Lord God of Hosts!
Heaven and earth are full of Thee,
Heaven and earth are praising Thee,
  O Lord most high.

Mary A. Lathbury (1877)

DOXOLOGY

Praise God, from whom all blessings flow
Praise Him, all creatures here below;
Praise Him above, ye heavenly hosts
Praise Father, Son, and Holy Ghost.

Bishop Thomas Ken (1637-1711)

FORGIVE ME, LORD

Forgive me, Lord, for Thy dear Son
The ill that I this day have done,
That with the world, myself, and Thee,
I, ere I sleep, at peace may be.

Bishop Thomas Ken (1637-1711)

83

FAIREST LORD JESUS

Fairest Lord Jesus
   Ruler of all nature,
O Thou of God and man the Son;
   Thee will I cherish, Thee will I honour,
Thou, my soul's glory, joy, and crown.

Fair are the meadows,
   Fairer still the woodlands,
Robed in the blooming garb of spring;
   Jesus is fairer, Jesus is purer,
Who makes the woeful heart to sing.

Fair is the sunshine,
   Fairer still the moonlight,
And all the twinkling, starry host:
   Jesus shines brighter, Jesus shines purer,
Than all the angels heaven can boast.

Anonymous Minister (1667)

FATHER, HEAR THE PRAYER WE OFFER

Father, hear the prayer we offer:
Not for ease that prayer shall be,
But for strength, that we may ever
Live our lives courageously.

Not for ever by still waters
Would we idly, quiet stay;
But would smite the living fountains
From the rocks along our way.

Be our strength in hours of weakness,
In our wand'rings be our guide;
Thro' endeavor, failure, danger,
Father be Thou at our side.

Let our path be bright or dreary,
Storm or sunshine be our share;
May our souls in hope unweary
Make Thy work our ceaseless prayer.

L. M. Willis

LORD, SPEAK TO ME

Lord, speak to me that I may speak
In living echoes of Thy tone;
As Thou has sought, so let me seek
Thine erring children, lost and lone.

O strengthen me, that while I stand
Firm on the Rock and strong in Thee,
I may stretch out a loving hand
To wrestlers with the troubled sea.

O teach me, Lord, that I may teach
The precious things Thou dost impart;
And wing my words that they may reach
The hidden depths of many a heart.

O fill me with Thy fullness, Lord,
Until my very heart o'erflow;
In kindling tho't and glowing word,
Thy love to tell, Thy praise to show.

Frances R. Havergal

NOW THE DAY IS OVER

Now the day is over, Night is drawing nigh;
Shadows of the evening, Steal across the sky.

Jesus, give the weary, Calm and sweet repose;
With Thy tend'rest blessing, May our eyelids close.

Grant to little children, Visions bright of Thee;
Guard the sailors tossing, On the deep blue sea.

Thru the long night watches, may Thine angels
    spread
Their white wings above me, Watching round my
    bed.

When the morning wakens, Then may I arise
Pure and fresh and sinless in Thy holy eyes.

Sabine Baring-Gould (1834-1924)

WE'RE MARCHING TO ZION

Come, we that love the Lord, And let our joys be
   known;
Join in a song with accord, Join in a song with
   sweet accord
And thus surround the throne, And thus surround
   the throne.

The hill of Zion yields, A thousand sacred sweets
Before we reach the heav'nly fields, Before we reach
   the heavn'ly fields
Or walk the golden streets, Or walk the golden
   streets.

Then let our songs abound, And ev'ry tear be dry;
We're marching thru Immanuel's ground,
We're marching thru Immanuel's ground
To fairer worlds on high, To fairer worlds on high.

                                    Isaac Watts (1674-1748)

Part V

Prayers for Holidays

NEW YEAR'S DAY

As we gather around the festive table this beautiful New Year's Day, we thank You, dear Lord, for Your goodness to us, and pray that the hungry everywhere may be fed. Be with us during this day and this year, guide and keep us. We ask this in His name. Amen.

Another year has dawned upon us. We greet this day with gratitude and thanksgiving in our hearts. Inspire us to be useful and effective throughout the coming days. We bless Your name. Amen.

NEW YEAR'S POEM

Another year is dawning!
  Dear Father, let it be
In working or in waiting
  Another year with Thee!
Another year of leaning
  Upon Thy loving breast,
Another year of trusting,
  Of quiet, happy rest.

Another year of service,
  Of witness for Thy love;
Another year of training
  For holier work above.
Another year is dawning!
  Dear Father, let it be
On earth, or else in heaven,
  Another year for Thee.

Frances R. Havergal (1874)

EPIPHANY

Heavenly Father, as You guided the wise men of old, direct us and bless us as we receive this blessing of food in Your name. Amen.

ASH WEDNESDAY

You, Lord, are our strength. We need Your forgiveness. On this day of penitence, draw near and help us to be thankful for Your sacrificial love. We are grateful for this meal and for Your boundless grace. Through Jesus Christ our Lord. Amen.

PALM SUNDAY

We rejoice in the kingship of our Savior. We pray that we may be blessed with His humility. We are grateful, Father, for this blessing of sustaining love that we are to receive in Your name. Amen.

MAUNDY THURSDAY

Our Father, as we recall the meaning of the Last Supper of our Lord with His disciples, our hearts are warmed by His humbleness. Bless us with that spirit as we partake of this meal. We praise You for His example and His redemptive work. In His name we pray. Amen.

GOOD FRIDAY

Merciful and everlasting God, we thank You for giving Your only Son, and delivering Him up for us all that He might bear our sins upon the cross. Fill our hearts with steadfast faith in Him so that we may not fear the power of any adversaries. Through the same Jesus Christ, our Lord we pray. Amen.

Our Father, we bow with heavy hearts when we think of the sacrificial love of our blessed Savior. We think now of Golgotha and the cross which He bore for us. Help us to live in His forgiving presence. We thank You now for Your unending love. In the Master's name. Amen.

EASTER

Dear Lord, on this day of special celebration for the resurrection of our Lord, we praise You for His victory over death. Thank you for the promise of eternal life that we have in You. Thank You for Your Son and His life here on earth. We are humbled because He was willing to die on the cross for our sins. Help us always to be mindful of that sacrificial love. Be with us as we strive to live to be worthy of the final resurrection which we will have with You. For we pray in the blessed Savior's name. Amen.

Joyfully, this Easter day,
I kneel, a little child, to pray,
Jesus, who hath conquered death,
Teach me, with my every breath,
To praise and worship Thee.

Sharon Banigan

MOTHER'S DAY

Dear Lord, we have set aside this day to honor our mother. We thank you for her unselfish love and devotion to our family. We thank You for her patience and her work which makes our home more loving and comfortable. Help us to remember continually to show our love and appreciation for her and all she does. Please be with her as she continues in her efforts to follow Your word and to be a good example. For we pray in Christ's name. Amen.

MEMORIAL DAY

O God, we thank You that You have preserved for us a nation with liberty and justice. Help us this day to honor the men who fought and died for our country. We thank You for the spirit of patriotism which binds us together. Grant that all in our nation may serve You first and foremost. Amen.

PENTECOST

Almighty and most merciful God, grant, we beseech Thee, that by the indwelling of Thy Holy Spirit, we may be enlightened and strengthened for Thy service; through Jesus Christ our Lord. Amen.

Book of Common Prayer

Come, O Holy Spirit, replenish the hearts of Thy faithful believers, and kindle in them the fire of Thy love, Thou that through manifold tongues hast gathered together all dissension and discord out of Thy holy church, and make us to be of one mind and unfeigned love, without which we cannot please Thee. Amen.

Coverdale

FATHER'S DAY

Our Father in heaven, on this day we honor our earthly father. We praise you for our family and all that it means to us. We thank you for the wisdom and leadership which our father provides for us. We are grateful for his hard work and determination which bring us so many opportunities. Please help our family to appreciate and love him. Give him strength and power to continue in his work for You. In Jesus' name we pray. Amen.

INDEPENDENCE DAY

Gracious Father, we thank You for freedom and its meaning in this good land. Help us to preserve it for every person on earth. With gratitude we eat this food. In Your name. Amen.

INDEPENDENCE DAY

> Our father's God, to Thee
> Author of liberty,
>   To Thee we sing:
> Long may our land be bright
> With freedom's holy light:
> Protect us by Thy might,
>   Great God, our King.

Samuel F. Smith

LABOR DAY

Lord, we know that You are the source of all of our blessings. We thank You for this food and for all the men and women whose hard work has made it possible for us to have it so conveniently. We are grateful for the opportunity to work and to provide for ourselves and those we love. We thank You now for the abundance of blessings which You have bestowed on us. Please be with those who are less fortunate than we are, and help us to share the fruits of our labor with them. For we pray through Christ. Amen.

THANKSGIVING

Dear Lord, today we are mindful of the countless blessings which You have given us. We are grateful for our country in which we have the freedom to worship You as we see fit. Lord, we praise You for Your handiwork, for the beauty of nature, and for the enjoyment that it brings us. As we come together to eat this food, help us to make this, and every day, a day of thanksgiving to You. We pray this through Your Son. Amen.

Lord, on this day of thanksgiving, we come to You to praise You for all that you have so generously given us. We know that all we have comes from You. We pray that You will help us not to be envious of what others have, but to be humbly grateful for the blessings we possess. Be with us now in our feast of thanksgiving, and keep us always humble in Your sight. In Jesus' name we pray. Amen.

THANKSGIVING

For flowers so beautiful and sweet,
For friends and clothes and food to eat,
For precious hours, for work and play,
We thank Thee this Thanksgiving Day.

For father's care and mother's love,
For the blue sky and clouds above,
For the springtime and autumn gay,
We thank Thee this Thanksgiving Day.

For all Thy gifts so good and fair,
Bestowed so freely everywhere,
Give us grateful hearts we pray,
To thank Thee this Thanksgiving Day.

Mattie M. Renwick

101

ADVENT

Almighty God, we thank You for the promise of a Savior so long ago. Prepare our hearts to accept Him anew in the spirit of love and peace which He brought into the world. Give us a true understanding of the meaning of Christmas and renew our spirits as we enter this holy season. Through Jesus Christ, our Lord. Amen.

CHRISTMAS EVE

Our Father, in the light of the guiding star, we bow at Bethlehem's cradle. Our hearts are warmed by the happy faces of little children. We are grateful for Your gift of the Christ child whom we adore. We pray in His name. Amen.

CHRISTMAS

Lord, we thank You that You sent Your only Son to this world to reveal Your plan for us. As we celebrate the day of His birth, we ask that You will be with all of Your children everywhere and bless them. Thank You for all the gifts that You have bestowed upon us. Keep us humble and guide us as we try to be more like Christ. We praise You for Your unending love. It is through Your blessed Son that we pray. Amen.

Eternal God, who sent Your only Son to save us from our sins, we thank You for His coming. We thank You for the joys of this holiday season, and we pray that You will be with us in all of our celebrations. Help us to remember that it is only because of Your love that we have such joy. Thank You for Christ and the promise of salvation He brought to the world on that first Christmas. In His holy name we pray. Amen.

CHRISTMAS

Lord, for the joys of Christmas, for the love of our family, for the gifts You have given us, for the freedom of our country, and for the food set before us, we give You thanks. As we remember Christ's birth, we are grateful for Your generosity in sending Him to this earth. Bless us as we eat, and be with all of those who are traveling during this holiday season. We ask this in Jesus' name. Amen.

Grant, we beseech Thee, almighty God, that the new birth of Thine only-begotten Son in the flesh may set us free who are held in the old bondage under the yoke of sin. Through the same Jesus Christ Thy Son, our Lord who liveth and reigneth with Thee and the Holy Spirit, ever one God, world without end. Amen.

Martin Luther (1533)

104

CHRISTMAS

What can I give Him
  Poor as I am?
If I were a shepherd
  I would bring a lamb,
If I were a wise man
  I would do my part;
Yet what can I give Him—
  Give Him my heart.

Christina Rossetti

How silently, how silently,
The wondrous gift is given;
So God imparts to human hearts
The blessing of His heaven.

Phillips Brooks

105

NEW YEAR'S EVE

We pause to give thanks for Your goodness to us, Father. You have brought us on our way to the end of another year. You have blessed us with food and surrounded us with Your constant love. Receive our humble thanks in the Master's name. Amen.

Thanks be to You, Lord Jesus,
For another year,
To serve You
To love You,
And to praise You. Amen.

Part VI

Prayers for Special Occasions

BIRTH

Lord, we praise You for the gift of life. We offer You humble thanks for this precious child whom You have entrusted to our care. We know that the family is the most important earthly institution which You have established, and we pray that You will guide us in making our home the place of love and understanding that You would have it to be. Please bless this child with health and strength, and help us to provide the proper spiritual training. We want this child to be like Jesus and to grow "in wisdom and stature, and in favor with God and man." For we pray through His name. Amen.

BIRTHDAY

Father, we praise You that as the years pass, each one brings new blessings and joys. You have been generous with us throughout all our lives, and we are truly grateful. Now we thank You for the joy of birthday celebrations, for the blessings of the year that has passed, and for the hope and anticipation of the year to come. May each birthday find us closer to You. We pray in the Savior's name. Amen.

> I ask and wish not to appear
>   More beauteous, rich or gay;
> Lord make me wiser every year,
>   And better every day.
>
> Charles Lamb (1775-1834)

WEDDING

Lord, we thank You for the holiness of marriage and all that it represents. We come before You now to ask Your special blessing on the two people who will be married today. Grant that they will remain firm in their total commitment to each other and to You. Give them patience and understanding and help them to put You above all things. Please bless their new home and make it a place of peace and happiness. We thank You for Your continuing care for all of Your children. We pray through Jesus. Amen.

Dear God, bless these two hearts as they blend into one. Grant that their marriage will be holy in Your sight. Make them grateful to You for all their joys and dependent on You in all their trials. Bring them closer to each other and to You. In Christ's name we pray. Amen.

ANNIVERSARY

Dear Lord, we praise You for the institution of marriage. We thank You that You have given us these precious years of life together. We are grateful that You have brought us through the trials as well as the joys of marriage and have given us so many of Your wonderful blessings. Help us always to remember the importance of our commitment to each other and to You. Help us to be patient, kind, and considerate with each other. Please continue to guide us in our efforts to make our home a place of love and peace. Be with us now on our special day and throughout our lives. In Jesus' blessed name we pray. Amen.

GRADUATION

Dear Lord, we thank You for the privilege of education. We are grateful that You have brought this graduate to the successful completion of this time of study. Thank You for the work done to accomplish this goal, for the guidance from the faculty and the administration, for the encouragement from family and friends, and for the sacrifices the parents have made to make this day possible. Please bless all graduates and help them to use the knowledge You have given them to further Your cause and to glorify You. Lord, please help all of us to conduct ourselves with integrity throughout the remainder of our lives and to rely on Your guidance in our pursuit of excellence. In the Savior's name. Amen.

BAPTISM

Our Father, we praise You for Your promise of salvation and Your willingness to let Your Son die on the cross for our sins. We thank You for this one who has become a member of Your kingdom. Please be with all of us who have chosen to follow You. Help us truly to die to our old selves and put on Christ in our new lives. Grant us strength and courage to continue in our faith and service to You. We pray in the blessed Savior's name. Amen.

ILLNESS

Eternal Father, strong to save! We come to You
now asking You to be with our loved one in this
time of illness. Please comfort him and restore his
health if it is Your will. Give him strength and faith
in You. Be with the doctors who attend him and
give them wisdom. For we pray in Jesus' name.
Amen.

Lord, please be with us when we are sick. Please
give us patience and the sure knowledge of Your
strength and comfort. We thank You for all those
who care for us. We pray that You will restore us to
health and to the service of Your kingdom. In
Christ's name. Amen.

DEATH

O God of eternal life, today we are surrounded by the evidences of death. We are once again reminded of the brevity of life. We are sad at the passing of this loved one, but help us to remember that there is a world far greater than this which comes after death. Please comfort us in our mourning, and be with us as we strive to live the remainder of our lives for You. For we pray in the name of the One who died for us. Amen.

VISITORS IN THE HOME

As we gather around this table, we render heart-felt thanks to You for the guests who join our family circle. And we pray as we eat this food together that our hearts may be filled with praise to You for this provision of Your love. Amen.

We thank You, our heavenly Father, for these guests who are gathered around this table. Strengthen the bond of our friendship as we partake of this provision for our bodies. Amen.

We thank You for the joy of friends and for the fellowship that graces this house. Give us grateful hearts for all Your tender care over us. Amen.

FAMILY REUNION

We praise you for bringing us together again as a family, and we ask Your blessing on this time we share. We thank You for the love and kinship that bind us together. We know that wherever we may be, we are a part of Your family. Now as we eat this meal together, we acknowledge all Your gifts to us and pray that we will remember You as the giver of every good and perfect gift in the days ahead. Be with us now and in the days ahead when we are apart. In Christ's name we pray. Amen.

FIRST DAY OF SCHOOL

Lord, we thank You for the opportunity to receive an education. As we start the year, help us to be receptive to new ideas and willing to work to accomplish worthwhile goals. Please be with our teachers and give them wisdom and patience in their dealings with us. In all that we study and do, Lord, help us to glorify You. In the Savior's name we pray. Amen.

117

FAMILY MEMBER ABSENT

Gracious Lord, as we come before You with thanks for all Your gifts which You have so generously given us, we ask Your blessing on our loved one who is absent from us. Please grant safety, health, and the sure sense of Your presence in all that is undertaken. Be with all of us until we can be together again. Thank You for Your continued guidance and love. In Jesus' name we pray. Amen.

TRAVEL

Dear Lord, we know that You are present everywhere. We know that wherever we may go that You will be there also. We ask You now to be with us as we travel. Please protect us from danger and guide us to our destination. Help us to trust You to watch over us wherever we are and please bring us safely home again. In Christ's name we pray. Amen.

NEW HOME

Lord, we come to You now asking that You bless us in our new home. We pray that You will help us to work together to make it a place of love, warmth, and happiness. Surround us with Your tender care and protect us from harm. We pray that all will be able to see the evidences of Your love in our home. Be with us in our efforts to glorify You. In Christ's name we pray. Amen.

WEEKEND

Dear heavenly Father, bless us as we seek rest and relaxation this weekend. Grant that we may be refreshed by the change in our activities. Please keep us from harm and bring us safely into another week to serve You. Thank You for your continuing care for us. In Jesus's name. Amen.

PICNIC

Lord, as we are surrounded by Your handiwork, we praise You for its beauty. We thank You for the glory of nature and of this day. We see Your evidences in all that is around us, and we are mindful of Your amazing love for us. We are thankful for the changing of the seasons and the joy that each one brings to our lives. Be with us now as we eat this food, and accept our praise and thanks for Your generosity toward us. In the Savior's name we pray. Amen.

SABBATH

Our Father, We thank You for this Sabbath day which You have given us to worship You. Be with us now as we prepare our hearts and minds to worship You. We ask Your forgiveness for our failures this past week, and we ask Your guidance for the coming week as we try to live more like Christ. Help us always to be mindful of Your love for us. In the Savior's name. Amen.

O God who makest us glad with the weekly remembrance of the glorious resurrection of Thy Son our Lord. Vouchsafe us this day such blessing through our worship of Thee, that the days to come may be spent in Thy service; through the same Jesus Christ our Lord. Amen.

Book of Common Prayer

PRAYER FOR THE NATION

Almighty God, in whose righteous will all things are and were created; You have gathered our people into a great nation and have given them the treasures of the land and of the sea. Make us reverent in the use of freedom, just in the exercise of power, and generous in the protection of the weak. Bless the president of the nation and all in authority. To our legislators and local representatives give insight and faithfulness, that our laws may clearly speak the right and our judges purely interpret it. May wisdom and knowledge be the stability of our times and our deepest trust be in You, the Lord of nations and the only righteous sovereign of men. Amen.

POEM FOR THE NATION

Lord, while for all mankind we pray,
   Of every clime and coast,
O hear us for our native land—
   The land we love the most.

O guard our shores from every foe;
   With peace our borders bless;
With prosperous times our cities crown,
   Our fields with plenteousness.

Unite us in the sacred love
   Of knowledge, truth, and Thee;
And let our hills and valleys shout
   The songs of liberty.

Lord of the nations! thus to Thee
   Our country we commend;
Be thou her refuge and her trust,
   Her everlasting friend.

            John R. Wreford (1837)

Our Family's
Own Special
Prayers